HOW TO EFFECTIVELY FIGHT STREESS

AND

LIVE A NORMAL LIFE

AGAIN

ANGELO ONEKA

TABLE OF CONTENTS

CHAPTERS

CHAPTER ONE

MONEY RELATED STRESS

WHAT MONEY HAS BECOME

Money has become almost everything in everybody's life. Everything we do these days requires money. One needs money for clothing, for shelter, for food, for treatments, for education, and the list goes on and on endlessly.
To have no money these days is like living without the heart.

MONEY PROBLEMS

Money problems have also become very rampant these days. Many people are without money. They strive to make ends meet. The money the majority people make is not enough to cater for their needs and requirements. Actually in most cases before one receives the salaries or the wages, that money is already spent. One just becomes a mere conveyor belt, receiving and passing it on straight away. That is why these days you hear the common saying ' I just work to pay my bills'. It is however very unfortunate that one goes to work just to pay bills. It is like a punishment. Who would want to be born in this world just for the purpose of paying bills? Sad as it is it has become a reality in many people's lives. Normally when I hear people say that, it sends me sick because that notion is dead end.

STRESSED OUT

Many people are stressed out because of lack of money. There are those who are in arrears of their rents and they do not have any clue where the money is going to come from in order to clear these arrears. This problem causes them to have sleepless nights. Some develop serious complications as a result of this.
Others have no food to put on the table, yet they have kids to feed. Some can not even pay their bills. And this may lead to termination of services including the very vital ones. When any of these happens, you are bound to be stressed out. A continuous failure to meet your obligation follow by subsequent terminations of services may also send you into deep depression. And when these happen to you, they will dawn on you for a very long time because depression is not easy to treat and is a complete nuisance that continuously attacks you without notice and mercy.

THE AMOUNT ONE GETS

The amount of money one gets is not very important but is how you spend your money that is quite critical. You may be making tons of money, yet you are constantly broke because you are a big spender. Yet one may be making little money but is very thrifty thus has money always.
In the latter paragraphs, I will show you how to avoid unnecessary spending and also avoid financial related stress.

SOLUTIONS

There are always solutions to every problem. And here are the solutions to the financial problems you may be encountering:

If lack of money is causing you stress, consider ways that would make for you money. One of the ways would be to have a second job or a business. Any one of these could generate for you some extra income that would alleviate your stress.

Always spend wisely.

Do not buy expensive items merely to show off.

Always keep yourself within the budget. Do not buy anything outside the budget.

Buy cheap nice things. Do not be fooled that cheap things are not good. If they look good who would know whether you bought them so cheaply.

Avoid buying things from the stores on main streets. They are too expensive for nothing.

Before you buy, always shop around and compare prices.

Do not be in competition with anyone, or you will be lured or forced to spend all your money, just because you want to look better than the one you are competing with.

Do not go to buy your groceries from expensive stores, they will make your money go fast. Food is food no matter where you buy it from, so long as the hygiene is of the required standard. You do not need to show off by going to expensive stores. If you do you will definitely suffer the consequences. You will always have no money, and stress will surely kick in.

Do not buy things you do not need just because of competition, the result is always disastrous. You will always be broke because you are buying things you cannot afford.

Avoid depending on credit cards, because it is easy to spend but very hard to pay back. Credit cards are very luring to spending, because this is easy money, it is not your money and spending becomes very easy. But when the creditors begin to harass you when you are unable to pay, it will cause you serious stress.

Avoid friends who would lure you to spend more.

Avoid going shopping with rich friends who are able to spend any amount of money while you are only able to buy only one or two items. This will stress you out and may turn you against your family.

Avoid creating so many bills.

Do not always authorize preauthorized payments to avoid financial problems and stress. You may do it now but way down the road you may be unable to meet your obligation and create more debts for yourself. Know that each time your payment does not go through, the bank or the financial institution you are dealing with will charge you for the no sufficient funds. And if this goes on for a long time you may find yourself with insurmountable debt.

Always count your blessings and know that you are far better off than so many others.

CHAPTER TWO

RELATIONSHIP RELATED STRESS

Relationship of any type is not always easy to handle. One has to be very careful in handling a relationship. It is a give and take situation. It is never a one way street. If you try a one way street relationship, you will never last in that kind of relationship. You must love to be loved. Do not think of always being loved one sided. You must give back love for love.

As we have just seen, relationship is not an easy thing to handle. There are bound to be problems in any relationship. Good or bad partners, there will always arise problems. Problems that come on a daily basis will always stress you out. However, you always need clear cult solutions to handle any problem. Be it big or small you need to handle them carefully and amicably.

ALWAYS BE DIPLOMATIC

Being soft is not a weakness but is strength. Even if you know that you are right and the other party thinks that you are wrong, be diplomatic in your disagreement with him or her. This will arrest any volatile situation. What you need is peace in the family even if you lose the argument. What good will it do to you to win the argument and have no peace in the relationship. Admit whatever it is for the sake of peace but make sure that you drive the point home at another convenient time. At that time, tell him or her outright that you meant what you said earlier on at the start of the argument, but you gave in merely for peace.

HONESTY

Honesty in any relationship is very important. Where there is no honesty, there will always be problems. And that relationship is bound to fall apart. Remember nobody goes into relationship to experience dishonesty. If you are practicing dishonesty, you are merely asking for problems. Do not let your beauty or handsomeness deceive you, yes people look for beauty and handsomeness but beauty or handsomeness without morale is a total sham. No body, let me repeat again nobody on the planet will stay in a relationship that full of immorality. Beauty and handsomeness is a deception. Have you ever wonder why handsome guys marry ugly ladies and why beautiful ladies marry ugly men? Most of the time, it is because of morality. Know that even if you are so beautiful or very handsome and you lack morale values you will always be churned at people will always take you for a joke. Both men and women always look for trustworthiness in the absence of that, there is always no relationship.

When you are dishonest, you are creating problems and stress both for yourself and your partner. Why do you choose that evil way that will only destroy you? Besides, you are also destroying your relationship or marriage.

DO NOT LISTEN TO NEGATIVE ADVICE FROM OTHERS

In your trouble that you have created by being dishonest to your partner, you will turn to friends for advice. Mark you, not all the advice you will get from these so called friends will be fruitful. Some will be sugar coated bullets ready to kill you. You must know, not all the friends are good friends, some are devils ready to bury you alive.

It is always better to solve your problems by yourself, I mean you and your partner rather than running around trying to get worthless advice from others, including those who call themselves experts. You may find that the so called experts are not even capable of solving their family problems. As it is said "how can a blind man lead another blind man?". By getting advice from your friends or so, you may make yourself more stressed out. Some of these friends may just want to destroy your marriage or your relationship. You are not a kid and you know the difference between right and wrong. So why don't you tell the difference? If you are wrong admit it and make necessary adjustments accordingly rather than look for worthless advice. Admit your wrong, and move on and get rid of this killing stress.

Sometimes even if you are right, you have to give peace a space in your relationship. By doing so, you are not only providing peace in your family but you are also getting rid of the stress and accordingly preserving your life. You are also preserving your relationship. Do not be fooled by anybody, your relationship is very important, especially those that have witnessed the test of time. If however, you hurriedly try to get rid of this relationship you will greatly regret later on and also realize too late that you made a mistake. No matter how bad he or she may be, but you are already used to one another. By taking this miscalculated move, you will be stressed out more as you think of her or him. If you really love one another, you will always find a solution to your disturbing problem however big it may be and enjoy your relationship again.

DO NOT BE FOOLED BY OTHER MEN OR WOMEN

Men always want to play game with any beautiful they see. Does that mean they are serious? No they are not. After getting what they want from you, they will forget you. If they do not forget you immediately, they may use you for a little while before dumping you. And if this secret love affair happens to destroy your marriage and you think he is going to welcome you in his house, forget it. He will never make you if wife because he has learnt who you are and he does not want to experience the same problem with another man. He will not accommodate you in his life because you are cheap and a problem. Why should he trust you anyway when you showed no trust to your partner?

There are women there too who are also ready to destroy your marriage. They will do everything to destroy your marriage. Do not be fooled by such women, stick to your wife. What else do you need, is she not a woman?

To avoid falling into troubles and more stress, always learn to say no and stick to your partner. If you do this when he or she is not around, one day he or she will learn of your unspoken trustworthiness and he or she will love you more than diamond. You will be his or her real sweetheart and you will have a total stress-free relationship. The love between you will also bloom.

SOMETIMES CALL A SPADE A SPADE

Sometimes to get to the core of problems and to realistically solve the problems, you have to be frank. Do not beat about the bush, just call a spade a spade and let the problems be solved once and for all. It may be a bitter truth but you are looking for a solution anyway.

BE READY ALWAYS TO DISCUSS ISSUES OPENLY

Discussions of problems work like medication. If you discuss your problems, then you will be able to solve your problems. Alternatively, if you do not discuss your problems openly, you are just like a farmer who cuts the stems of the carrot to make the carrot grow bigger. Hiding problems in your heart will only worsen your current problems. And one day, you are going to explode like an atomic bomb and utterly destroy your relationship.

Know that words spoken in anger, has no substance, and most of the times are very destructive. They sting like the bees and hurt like a toothache. Be very careful with whatever words you speak in anger. Instead bring the problem to the fore for friendly and serious discussion, and totally uproot the problem once and for all. Never, never hide problems in your heart, let you partner know of it, you may be right, you may also be wrong. Bring forth the problem and let him or her defend herself or himself. And always be willing to accept sincere apology and any meaningful explanation. Who knows, you may also make a similar mistake in the future.

ALWAYS AVOID EXPLODING
Do not become an atomic bomb of the relationship. Learn to be calm and diplomatic always. That way, you will be able to solve any problem. However, if you explode, the other guy may also explode and the relationship will automatically be shattered into debris that can never be fitted back. Always avoid that kind of behaviour and sustain the relationship. Remember any problem can be solved so long as both parties are willing to listen to one another, also ready to admit their faults and also willing to forgive one another.

However, forgiveness should not always be abused by the guilty party, by intentionally doing or committing the same act over and over again. This kind of behaviour is an insult to the already injured party. Avoid it altogether and eliminate stress from the family. Remember, we marry to love and not to fight. Marriage should not become a war zone rather it should be a paradise where love blooms.

SOLUTIONS TO STRESS
Be honest to your partner not to create stress in the relationship.

Be diplomatic always in discussing your problems with your partner. It will quell the situation and provide room for peace and deter stress.

Do not seek advice from friends, they can only make you be stressed out more, rather solve your problems with your partner.

Avoid going with other men, they will only create problems for you and thereby cause you more stress.

Avoid going with other women, they will destroy your marriage.

Admit sometimes that your partner is right even if you know that he is wrong, just to create peace and to eliminate the oncoming stress.

Do not hurry to get out of the relationship. It will cause you more stress, rather work out any existing problem amicably.

Know that every family has some kind of problems, but those who work out their problems stay almost stress-free and their families stick.

Always avoid exploding in order not to aggravate the problems.

Always be ready to discuss your problems with your partner.

Treat every problem with calm.

Always be frank with your partner, call a spade a spade to help solve the problems and eliminate stress from the relationship.

Never hide any problem in your heart. It will only create more problems and possibly worse ones.

CHAPTER THREE

SICKNESS RELATED STRESS

Sickness or illness can always have serious effects on one's life. This becomes even worse when you are constantly in pains. It stresses you out and sometimes you may become completely depressed. As a result of what affects your health, it makes life meaningless and not worth living. Life thus becomes more of a punishment rather than enjoyment. Different kinds of sickness will always send out different messages.

DIFFERENT KINDS OF SICKNESS

There are always different kinds of sickness in the world that afflict people. There are those sicknesses that can easily be treated. And there are those that may take a long time to be treated. Yet there are those that are very complicated and chronic. These ones may not be treated at all. All these sicknesses send different signals to the patients. Patients with treatable sicknesses, normally have hope, and are therefore less stressed out. Those that are afflicted with somewhat complicated sicknesses that may require prolonged treatments are normally stressed out as they worry whether they are going to be better or their sickness may not leave them. Yet there are those with very complicated sicknesses. Sicknesses that may never be treated at all because they are chronic. Cancer is one of those sicknesses. This category of patients, are not only stressed out but also constantly worry about dying.

WORRY NOT BECAUSE YOU CAN BE HEALED

Whether you have a chronic sickness do not let it stressed you out because anything in life is possible. We have seen those that were near death completely healed and lived normal life again. We also read in The Bible of some people who were already ready to cross the river of death, yet got well because God wanted them still to live. Besides, we read about Lazarous who died and was raised back to life by The Lord Jesus Christ. Are you already dead? No, you are still alive and therefore do not lose hope. You still have hope and you can still live for many more years. This sickness can leave you too however chronic it may be. Just totally commit yourself to God Almighty and He may give you another chance. Do not worry. God can easily heal you. In your pain and in your sleep always talk to God and continuously ask Him for miraculous healing and believe it and He will surely do it for you. My friend God is power, do not lose hope. I know that you can live a normal life again by the power of
The Living God. Now stop worrying and know that God is God. This is not religion it is bare truth. I know you will get well again. God will heal you. It is time to live again. Now shake off the stress and shake off the sickness and let new life begin now.

OTHER SOLUTIONS

Seek for proper treatment.
Administer the medication as per the doctor's instructions so that you may get well and eliminate that stress.
Always have enough rest to recover.
Visit your doctor very often if you are not hospitalized so that you are able to get rid of this sickness and stress.
Have some exercise on a daily basis if you are still able to do that. This will help with stress.
If your sickness is not grounding you yet, always take a walk. It will do you a lot of good. It also

takes away the stress that you are currently experiencing.

Do not worry about that sickness, but believe that you are going to get well. This will not only help in removing the stress but will also bring about recovery.

Always try to be happy, it works wonders and is also a medicine to many health problems.

Leave your sickness or illness to God. He may heal you to the surprise of everyone.

Take a look at those who are in more dangers than you, and you will feel better.

Always occupy yourself with something to do in order to keep stress abbey.

CHAPTER FOUR

WORK RELATED STRESS

Work is one of the serious factors that cause stress. Work related stress could come from many factors such as the boss, management, co-workers, traveling to and from work, being late, the type of work, and the list goes on and on.

THE BOSS

Some of the bosses can turn out to be a complete problem. The boss may at times want you to do the things you do not want to do. Some of the bosses may even go beyond the requirements of their duties by demanding sex from their employees. And when such employees say no, they turn against them. They may decide to give such employees less hours thus depriving them of income. Or they may give very difficult tasks to such employees to perform. Yet still they may find ways to terminate such employees. This is totally illegal because no one has the rights to demands sex from his or her subordinates.

When this kind of thing happens in work places, a worker becomes totally stressed out. This becomes even acute whenever it is time to report for work. One is thus left discussing to herself or himself whether to go to work or not. This is a total nightmare that should be avoided at all costs and should also be reported to the authorities.

CO-WORKERS

Co-workers can also at times be a thorn in the flesh. They may make things difficult for you. They may also gossip about you once you are away, and the list goes on and on endlessly.

FALSELY REPORTING YOU TO THE BOSS

Many co-workers are not good people. You may find that many of them work as spies for their bosses. On many occasions they may falsely report their fellow workers to the bosses. They may make innocent people lose their jobs, which is totally wrong and evil. They also make the places of work very stressful. Besides, they may also cause conflicts between the workers.

Such people, who falsely report their co-workers, should themselves be fired as they cause moral of the workers to go down.

TYPE OF WORK

It is a known fact that many people do not like their work. They stay around in their jobs simply because they have no alternatives. Besides, they continue in their jobs because they have to feed their families. If all these factors were not tying them down, they would quit their jobs much easily.

Performing the job, that one does not like, always causes stress.

WAKING UP

Some people do not live near their work places. They live kilometers away from their work places. That therefore means that whenever they are going to work, they have to wake up very early in the mornings. They may also reach their homes late at nights because of the distance they have to travel. When they reach homes, they are already completely exhausted. And they have to go to beds straight away after their dinners, in order to wake up early in the mornings. They also have no time completely for their families except over the week-ends. This is a very stressful life.

TRAFFIC

Some workers normally witness serious stress because of the traffic. When they have to leave homes, they have to leave early enough if they have to avoid traffic nuisance and stress. If they leave at busy hours that mean that they will be caught up in real traffic jam. Being caught up in a traffic jam can be very stressful because of reaching late at work. If this trend continues on a daily basis and for a long time, it may result into mental problem.

SOLUTIONS ON WORK RELATED STRESS

If your boss is giving you problems, quit that job. Your life is more important than that job. If however you decide to stay, one day, you may become disabled because of stroke or heart attack that may result from the stress you are getting from this work.

If you do not have any qualification that will provide you a new job, consider going back to school to acquire necessary qualifications.

Re-locate closer to your place of work so that you do not have to wake so early in the mornings. This will give you time to sleep. Remember, sleep is very important for your health that is why God created it. Its absence would cause you many problems, including mental problem, if the trend is prolonged.

Whenever leaving for work, make sure you leave early to avoid traffic that could seriously give you stress.

Do not socialize with the workers whom you know act as spies for their bosses. This will eliminate any wrongful reports on you.

If you do not like your job, quit it, and find another job and save yourself from stress.

CHAPTER FIVE

EDUCATION RELATED STRESS

Education is not an easy task to accomplish and is not an easy thing to attain. It entails a lot of hard work, total dedication, time consuming and a lot of headache and stress. It can consume you both physically and mentally. Besides, it is not a one day job. It runs over many years to accomplish.

In education, there numerous factors, that can stress you out. Some of these factors are:

Homework
Studies
Having no time for fun
Fellow students
The teachers
The parents, and
Examinations and tests

HOMEWORK

Many students do not like homework. They feel that it deprives them of their leisure time when they should be relaxing and enjoying themselves. Besides, you may get an homework that you do not any clue how to do it. This becomes so distressful. In this case, one is then left to a serious disturbing decision to make. Should I do it or should I not do it and come up with an excuse? If you do it, everything may be wrong which will result into you being scolded by the teacher and also laughed at and minimized by your fellow students.

This is now both a physical and a mental problem to you. It is consuming you both mentally and physically and also driving you weak as you feel the direct effects in your body.

If you do not do it, the teacher may scold you too. Besides, he or she may still require you to finish it up in addition of the new given one. And if you keep on pilling them up, you will never be able to finish them up. This will surely stress you out the more and you may have sleepless nights because of them. If you are still under the care of your parents, they too may be on your neck.

STUDIES

Studying is not easy for some people, especially when you study and you do not absorb anything. It is very stressful. It becomes more annoying because you are putting in so many hours just for nothing. The great disappointment normally comes when a teacher pulls you in front of the class to narrate what you studied and what you know, and yet you understood nothing and know also nothing. Your peers will laugh at you and also call you a dummy. When this happens, you will feel totally demoralized.

HAVING NO TIME FOR FUNS

As you take your education seriously and want to succeed in the future, you find yourself totally consumed in studies that you have very little time or no time for funs. This may stress you out.

FELLOW STUDENTS

If you are doing so well at school or in your studies, you may become a laughing stock for your fellow students. This may further complicate your studies and stress you out. However, do not worry, always try to bury your head deep into studies and turn their scorn and laughter into success. If you are willing to study hard , you can always succeed, for everything in life is possible. We only need the right solutions and we have got the clue.

Prove your peers wrong. You can do it, if others can, you can too. Get out of stress, stress will only make you dull and you are not a dull girl or a dull boy. You too are bright except that you did not apply yourself completely. Do so now.

THE TEACHERS

Have the teachers become a problem to you because you are not doing so well? Prove them also wrong. Study hard and become one they did not know, the bright one. You can do it, surprise them and turn them into your friends. Do not worry and do not stress yourself out, but study. Who knows what future holds for you. You may become great and famous too, let nothing bother you and stress you out.

PARENTS

Are your parents also on your neck? Again I say study hard and surprise them. Make them proud of you.

EXAMS AND TESTS

Are these two things bothering you? Do not let them bother you. Study hard and master them. Put them under your feet. Again let me say, nothing is impossible. Everything can be overcome if we set our minds to overcome them. Look at how many people conquered Mount Everest! You too can conquer the exams and the tests, only you need to study hard.

SOLUTIONS

Do your homework promptly to avoid stress.

Always study hard to succeed in your studies, tests and examinations.

Always study hard to prove those who mock you and laugh at you wrong.

Always study hard to prove your teachers wrong.

Always study hard to succeed in life.

Always study hard to make your parents proud of you and avoid stress from them.

Always study hard to destroy stress from feeling that you are dull.

CHAPTER SIX

GAMBLING RELATED STRESS

Gambling can easily become an habit that may be very difficult to get rid of. It may also send you into serious stress. This stress may come because of different factors, such as:

> Losing
> Lack of money
> Loss of properties, and

Family problems

LOSING
When you gamble, you are bound to lose rather than win. Most of the time you will be losing and as a result you will be stressed out.

LACK OF MONEY
Since you gamble a lot and you often lose, you will thus be broke most of the time. This will totally complicate your life. You will be stressed out. You may also go into serious depression. This comes about because every time you get money, you go gambling and the probability of losing that money is always ninety nine percent.

LOSS OF PROPERTIES
Many gamblers have often lost their properties such as vehicles, houses etc, because after finishing all the money they have, in gambling, they then turn to their properties to realize money for gambling. Some think by continuous gambling, they may get their money back but normally the loss continues unabated. This means more stress as properties are lost in gambling. This may yet lead to more serious problem, family problem.

FAMILY PROBLEMS
As all the money is gone, vehicles are gone and the house or houses are gone into gambling, a new phase of life will emerge, family problems. The family will begin to fall apart because nothing is left except the human beings. These losses will create quarrels, fights, separation or even a divorce in the family. Sometimes these losses may also lead to suicide as the family becomes stressed out and depressed with no hope of life anymore.

SOLUTIONS
Do not gamble in order to avoid major problems and stress.
If you are already committed to gambling, pull out immediately.
If you are already addicted to gambling, seek help in order to stop it.
To avoid serious stress and problems, do not go for your properties.

CHAPTER SEVEN

SPORTS RELATED STRESS

You may become totally stressed out if you are not performing well in your sports activities, especially if you are already beginning to have some problems with the   management. Losses in sports especially may cause some stress especially if you had been doing well before.

SOLUTIONS

Always practice hard to improve and to gain back your glory.
Do not drink as this may destroy your capability.
Always remain fit so that you are not stressed out.
Always avoid smoking. Exercise a lot to be fit and ready for challenges.
Always eat well.
Do not use drugs they will destroy you and your career.

CHAPTER EIGHT

DRINKING RELATED STRESS

Drinking may also cause stress. The stress may come about because of the following:

> Lack of money
> Hangover
> Drinking induced sickness

LACK OF MONEY

If you are used to drinking every day, the day you do not drink, you may become stressed out and depressed. This may further worsen by the lack of money that drinking has caused. Now that you can not afford to buy drinks and food, will cause more stress.

HANGOVER

Hangover may also cause you some stress of any kind.

DRINKING INDUCED SICKNESS

Because you had been drinking too much and for a very long time, you may develop drinking related sickness such as problem with the liver. Always becoming a weakling and unable to do anything. The list of sickness may go on and on.

SOLUTIONS

If you drink have moderation.

Do not use all your money on drinks or you may become stressed out and depressed too.

Seek for counseling if drinking has become a problem.

CHAPTER NINE

DRIVING RELATED STRESS

Driving on busy roads can be very stressful. You have all kinds of drivers on the roads. Some drivers are good drivers while others are terrible drivers. You also have those driving under the influence of drugs while others under the influence of drinks. These two categories are more stressful to deal with and they are very dangerous in their driving.

You also have people who are actually late for their works and appointments. They want to drive as if they are the only road users. They cut in from every side of the roads not caring about other motorists.

These people who are late for works and appointments are normally fully stressed out as they drive. They feel that everyone on the roads are bad drivers, a nuisance and crazy, forgetting about themselves. By the time they reach their places of work or appointments, they are done as dinner.

You may also have other road users such as the pedestrians, the cyclists who will really vex you to the point of madness. Especially the cyclists on the roads riding where the traffic is, and slowing down the traffic. It is very annoying. And some pedestrians, crossing the roads as if the tortoise is the one crossing. They take their own time in disregard to other road users.

TRAFFIC JAM

Traffic jam is more stressful and very annoying. It makes you late for your job, appointments and everything. When you are caught in a traffic jam, you really feel stressed out. At times you feel like you should fly.

It is really very annoying especially on high ways where you cannot go ahead, cannot go back and cannot turn anywhere or change course. You are virtually left stuck on the steering wheel, fully stressed out. Sometimes despite the heavy traffic with nowhere to go, yet you some drivers honking as if they want you to fly. You wonder where they want you to go. They see traffic in front and at the sides and yet they continue honking.

TRAFFIC LIGHTS

Traffic lights are even more stressful especially when you are in a hurry and every traffic light you reach turns red.

OTHER MOTORISTS

Other motorists especially those aggressive and reckless ones can really be very annoying and stress you out. Some of these motorists have no regards for other motorists. They feel that they are the only ones on the streets. They like to cut in and they also like to honk even if they see that there is traffic ahead of you.

ANIMALS CROSSING THE ROADS
Sometimes in some places you may have animals constantly crossing the roads and slowing down the traffic. Some of these animals may take their time as they cross the roads in convoys. This can really be time consuming.

RAIL CROSSINGS
At times you may also have train drivers who can vex you up. When they come to where the road crosses the lines, they and deliberately stop at the crossing point just for sometime thereby tying down the traffic. This sends real stress to the motorists.

SOLUTIONS

Always leave your home early for work so that you do not have to rush, and also avoid stress. When you are using the highway, make sure that you leave early before the traffic hits the roads. Relocate near your work place so that you do not have to drive a long way. This will solve you a lot of problems such as stress and traffic nuisance.
If you are not going too far avoid using highways.
If you are using roads that have a lot of traffic lights, leave early for work or appointments.
Always prepare yourself mentally for any traffic nuisance.
Avoid following the trucks or being in front of them.
Always be calm no matter what situation is on the road to avoid stress and possible heart attack.

CHAPTER TEN

CRIME RELATED STRESS

Criminals as well as those who live with them normally get stress.

CRIMINALS
The criminals normally get stressed out because they feel that they are always being sought after by the authorities. They also feel stressed out by knowing that people are watching their movements. Also when they are planning to commit crimes, they get stressed out because they are not sure whether they are going to come out it clear or may be arrested or even killed. And once they have committed crimes, they get stressed out because of knowing that authorities are looking for them and that they might go behind bars. Everyday to them becomes so stressful. And when they have robbed, whenever they go to spend that money they become stressed out because they do not know whether they are going to be arrested. Their lives are always lives of uncertainty and stress.

NEIGHBOURS OF CRIMINALS

It is quite a terrible thing to live with criminals. Their presence makes life uncertain and very stressful because these are people who are bent on doing bad things always. It is their way of life.

CRIMINAL THIEF

If you live with criminal thieves, you always worry about your properties. Even when you go to bed, you are stressed out for you worry that they may break into your house to rob you. This makes life very uncertain. Your own properties have become quite a nightmare because of the presence of these criminals. You can also hardly sleep at night because of the burglary. All these will totally stress you out. Even for your very own life, you do not know whether it will be there the next day because of these evil people.

MURDERER

And if your neighbour is a murderer, that will surely send chills into your life. You begin to live a life of uncertainty for you do not know when this criminal is going to strike. That therefore always makes your life very stressful.

IF YOUR NEIGHBOUR IS A KIDNAPPER

If your criminal neighbour is a kidnapper and you have kids, your life will always be restless. You always worry about your kids being kidnapped by this criminal. Everyday you are totally stressed out and you become more stressed out whenever you see him or her. This stress also affects your kids. They are fearful of this monster and are forced to stay indoor without any freedom to play outside.

A CHILD MOLESTER NEIGHBOUR

A child molester neighbour will always send you into serious stress because of the fear that one day he may molest your child. Not only that, but he may also kill your child after molesting her. This feeling will always keep you stressed out.

SOLUTIONS

Re-locate from that place of the criminals.
Never leave your child alone at home as this may stress you out.
Install video cameras in and around your house to monitor any criminal activities.
report any suspicious activity to the authority.

CHAPTER ELEVEN

DRUG RELATED STRESS

Drugs are known to cause a lot of problems, such as mental problem, violence, becoming a vegetable, etc. They can never be a solution, but are always a source of problems. Drugs can destroy a person gradually as the usage continues. Many people however think the contrary of the truth, they think that drugs will solve their problems and possibly make them well. This a total farce. By using drugs on a continuous basis, a person is not only destroyed but also delays and multiplies his problems into the future.

Drugs related stress comes about when a person who constantly uses drugs is unable to secure drugs he or she uses on daily basis. This person will be stressed out. If this continues, it may turn into serious depression.

Inability to secure drugs because of lack of money may cause a person also to steal.

SOLUTIONS

Stop using drugs at all cost and live a normal life. Go to drug rehabilitation center in order to come out of drug usage and its after effects. Do not associate anymore with those who use drugs.

Re-locate from the area where you used to use drugs.

CHAPTER TWELVE

SOCIAL RELATED STRESS

It is always not very easy to get along with everyone. You may like some people while you also hate others because of what they do and what they say. Other people may also hate you while others may like you naturally.

It is always a very difficult thing to deal with people. There are some people who are naturally difficult to deal with while there some people who are easy to deal with and to also like.

PEOPLE WHO STRESS YOU OUT

There are people who by what they do and what they say will always stress you out. Whatever they say is always like you have been shot in the heart. It like they never ever digest whatever they say. They are always very provocative and very insulting in all their statements.

HABIT

Some habits in other people can also stress you out. These habits are quite numerous and I do not need to go into them. Again, it depends on what you like and what you do not like. Like the saying goes ' another man's meat is another man's poison'.

THE SOCIETY RELATED STRESS

Societies can also make you totally stressed out. Some of the habits that will really stress you out are being nosy. Some of these people want to know everything you do in life, and this can be very irritating. If it goes on for a long time and on a daily basis, it will definitely stress you out.

Some of them may even choose to tell lies about you. This is not only stressful but it also eats into your reputation, quite a damaging thing. And some people may just swallow those lies without even digesting them. Many people are unable to tell the difference between a lie and the truth. So whatever they hear remains the truth to them.

And then you have another category that will always pick up the fights with you.

FRIENDS RELATED STRESS

Some friends can really stress you out by what they say and what they do. Some of their statements, are without digestion, they come as if they are coming out of a child's mouth. Continued association with such people will surely have some health effects on you. They will stress you out.

Other friends may lie and gossip about you, but in your presence, they will always pretend to be very nice. Such friends are not only stressful but are also very dangerous. It is better to deal with someone who tells you something in your face rather than talk behind your back.

Then there are other friends who are envious of you and always want to have what you have. These are really not friends but are hidden enemies who are so destructive.

SOLUTIONS

Stay away from people who always make you annoyed.

Stay away from people whose habits irritate you.

Stay away from people who do not know how to control their tongues or their behaviour.

If you are living in a community that always stresses you out because of being nosy, and also telling lies about you, re-locate from the area to avoid all these problems.

Avoid and terminate any friendship with bad friends who lie and gossip about you.

Waste no time but get rid of those friends who always want to have what you have. These are very dangerous people. You would rather deal with the open enemies than with this type of people. This type of people are like cancer that destroys you without your knowledge, by the time you get to know that you have it, you are already a terminal patient. These types of friends are like that. They will corrode you just like that. Get rid of them as soon as possible.

CHAPTER THIRTEEN

THE IN-LAWS RELATED STRESS

On many occasions, the in-laws have always interfered into marriages. They have also caused untold sufferings to the marriages.

MOTHER -IN-LAW

A wrong mother in-law would always encourage her daughter to have an affair in this regard to the marriage. This kind of behaviour, has caused many families to fall apart. The worst mothers-in-law are those that practice prostitution. If you have a mother-in-law like that, you are in real serious problems. Your marriage will always rock like a boat that is being tossed by the storm. You will always have serious problems in your family which eventually may lead to a divorce and the suffering of your children.

FATHER-IN LAW AND MOTHER-IN-LAW
And if you have a father-in-law and mother-in-law from the husband's side, who do not like their daughter-in-law, that marriage is bound to have a lot of problems and a lot of stress too, will always rock around like a boat being tossed by the storm. If the man is weak an unprincipled, they may cause him to break up the marriage. On the other hand, if the man is strong and principled, then he will tell off. He may tell them he brought the lady to be his wife and not for his father or his mother. That should drive the point home, but some of them cannot easily give up. They may still continue to cause problems because the want to get rid of this girl.

BROTHER-IN-LAW
Some brothers in law are worse than the devil. They may tell their bothers to get rid of their wives and marry another woman. And the brothers-in-law from the wives' sides may engineer their sisters to quit the marriages for other men.
Both these steps are totally wrong and evil. Because The Bible says what God has joined together, let no man put asunder. Who then are these people with the rights to destroy marriages. They are either the devils or are the agents of the devil who are fighting God.

SISTERS-IN-LAW
Some sisters-in law from both sides can be as terrible as the devil. They may ask the brothers or the sisters to quit their marriages. The sisters are even more persistent in encouraging the break-ups of marriages.

SOLUTIONS
1. Do not listen to them, ignore them.
2. In order to get rid of stress coming from these people, if you are living in their house, move out immediately.
3. if you are living in the neighbourhood where they normally come around to your house, relocate immediately.
4. Tell them, that you married her or him for yourself and not for them and request them to leave you alone.
5 .Increase the love between you and your partner.
6.Do not visit them until they change their mentality.
7. When the write to you do not write to them.
8. When they call you, do not answer.
9. Always love your partner, no matter what. Know that if they destroy your marriage they will

not even help you instead they will blame you for breaking up your marriage.
10. Always stay away from trouble causing sisters.

CHAPTER FOURTEEN

FAMILY RELATED STRESS

Family related stress is very common. It arises from different factors. Some of these factor are:
>Spouses
>Children
>The relatives

SPOUSAL STRESS

Not everything in a marriage can be great. Although marriage is a great thing, yet there can arise problems at times because it is not possible that the two will always agree on every issue. There at times arise some disagreements. It is the norm of life. When two or more people live together, there are always diverse opinions. It is totally impossible that the two will all the time agree on different issues.

Disagreements are by no means a sign of no love. You can disagree on a number of different issues, yet you still remain great lovers.

HUSBAND RELATED STRESS

Sometimes, a husband can become a real headache. He may not totally agree with all your ideas or what you might be doing. This however, does not mean that there is no love. May be certain things you are doing may seem so brilliant to you but to your husband, it may be total stupidity. He may be right and he may also be wrong.

If he tells you that your idea is total garbage, do not disagree with him but rather re-examine what you are doing and if he is indeed right, go along with him ad if he is wrong the advance your points to him to convince him.

However, there are some husbands who can really be mean in everything. At most times, this happens when there is no longer any trace of love in the marriage. Everything that a wife does or says always turns into serious problems. Besides, there are always constant quarrels.

This kind of situation becomes even worse when a husband has friends that normally wrongly advice him. These friends, who are giving him wrong advice will always tell him all kinds of things and what to do. And if he is not wise enough will always implement the advice without analyzing it not knowing that these friends are misleading him and to destroy his family.

The worst problems come when the husband begins to have extra marital affairs. This woman or the women he is having an affair with begin to tell him all kinds of things including telling him to get rid of the wife.

Many unwise husbands quite often fall into that kind of trap only to realize later that he is after all wrong. But by then it may already be too late, the marriage has already been destroyed.

Extra marital affairs are very bad thing. It destroys families. By doing that you are virtually shooting your wife right in the heart. It is worse than the bullet; she does not die right away, but dies gradually, a slow and very painful death. Why do that to someone you love? This person is part of you.

This kind of problem will always cause serious stress to your wife. This is a stress that cannot easily go away. It is like a permanent scare. One may forget it for a little while but it bounces back always. This kind of problem can always send someone to the grave very fast.

WIFE RELATED STRESS

Some wives can be a real thorn in the flesh. They will cause you all sorts of problems. You solve one problem yet another one is in the making. They become a routine.

Others are naggers. They will nag you everyday that you feel that your heart is not beating anymore. Some of them do this unconsciously, while others do it intentionally to hurt you. Some are just born like that and you cannot really change them and all what you have to do is to adjust your own way and try to live with the situation.

The most disturbing thing that can cause one serious problem, is when one learns that a spouse is having an affair. This is a real headache that can cause one to become crazy if you do not handle it with care and promptly. In most cases people seek for immediate divorce although it is not a complete solution. That is just another nail in your rib. The stress from this becomes ongoing.

It is however totally wrong for one to indulge into extra marital affairs. It is a big insult.

CHILDREN'S RELATED STRESS

It is a blessing to have children. They make your life complete and you also feel proud to be a parent. However, there are children who will always send you crazy. They do things that are out of the norms of life. Some of the things they do will always irritate you or cause you real problems.

As long as they live with you, they will always cause you stress. That means you are dying slowly everyday.

SOLUTIONS

1 Be a real parent and ignore most of the things that they do that make you crazy. Try to live with those problems if you cannot rectify them.

2. Rectify this problem immediately.

3.Send the trouble causer to a boarding school if you can.

4.Give love to those children, may be that is what they are looking for.

5. Always discuss any problem frankly with your children.

       Stop doing what makes your husband mad at you.

       Ask your husband to stop his marital affairs immediately or else you leave.

       Be nice to your husband even if he is bad to you.

       Always show love. Love is a very powerful weapon.

       Seek proper family counseling if you cannot solve your problems.

       Avoid extra marital affairs.

Try always to live with the nagging.
Avoid extra marital affairs.
Go to the root cause of the problem, and completely uproot it.
Always have love in your heart. It is a great medicine.
Remove hate from your heart.
When you are wrong admit it and solve the problem promptly.

www.ingramcontent.com/pod-product-compliance
Lightning Source LLC
Chambersburg PA
CBHW072254310526
45795CB00011B/1140